The Nerves Centre

ANGELA SZCZEPANIAK

The Nerves Centre

a novel-in-performance-anxiety
in ten acts
131 stanzas
2417 phonetic utterances

LIVRES DC BOOKS

Cover illustration by Jamie Popowich.
Author photograph by Icon London.
Book designed and typeset by Primeau Barey, Montreal.
Edited by Jason Camlot.

Legal Deposit, Bibliothèque et Archives nationales du Québec
and Library and Archives Canada, 1st trimester, 2021.

Library and Archives Canada Cataloguing in Publication
Title: The nerves centre : a novel-in-performance-anxiety in ten acts, 131 stanzas, 2417 phonetic utterances / Angela Szczepaniak.
Names: Szczepaniak, Angela, 1975- author.
Description: Poems. | Includes index.
Identifiers: Canadiana 20200411942 | ISBN 9781927599532 (softcover)
Subjects: LCSH: Performance anxiety–Poetry.
Classification: LCC PS8637.Z39 N47 2021 | DDC C811/.6–DC23

For our publishing activities, DC Books gratefully acknowledges the financial support of SODEC and of the Government of Canada through Canadian Heritage and the Canada Book Fund. *Nous reconnaissons l'aide financière du gouvernement du Canada.*

Société de développement des entreprises culturelles Québec
Canada

Printed and bound in Canada.
Interior pages printed on Enviro Book, an environmentally responsible paper containing 100% post-consumer recycled fiber, processed chlorine-free and manufactured using biogas energy.
Distributed by LitDistCo.

DC Books
5 Fenwick Avenue
Montreal West, Quebec H4X 1P3
www.dcbooks.ca

Contents

Act 1

Act Natural, Be Yourself

speaker stands alone at microphone   pin-neat and polite

serenity slipping through finger twitches

speaker readies self opens mouth   silence

mouth opens   this time with resolve

silence snaps   jaws shut

speaker opens steadied mouth   finally

hhh hhh hh

h

hh h hhh h

regroup

reappoach

hhh

hhh ahhhhh

hhh

speaker backsteps   wheezes a casual graveyard whistle

shuffles a softshoe

sidles up   microphone adjacent

to take it by surprise

h h h h h h

h

h

hhh h h h h h h

h h h h h hhh

hhaaah

speaker runs a wide circle   figure-eights & pirouettes
back

to centrestage

pushes breezeblown sweatslick hair   from eyes

uhh haaa uhh haaa ha

uh

uhhhhh

hhhhp

hhhhhup

hhhhhup hhup

hhuuup

speaker tumbles expertly across stage

a series of technically precise somersaults & handsprings

sticks landing at microphone

p

p p p-hhuh

p-hhhh u p p-hh p-hh

p-hhhhah

p-hhh uup p-hh

p-hh p-hhh

p

p

speaker coughs   up   a string of single h's

pulls out a chain of sputtering h-h-h-h-h-h-h

stragglers catching in the cogs of   vocality p-hhh   up

p-hhh   uuuupppp   p-hup

p-hup   p-hup

hup

[*curtain*]

Act 2

Take a Walk, Jump Up & Down, Shake Out Your Muscles

speaker attempts crossing
to centrestage

lifts a foot

foot remains still

tries foot again   still foot still

other foot   still

still   feet still

speaker tries a leap

feet tie shoelaceish round each other
toe knots
ankle shot
knees pop

microphone–

defiant
three feet away
hit its neon tape mark just fine

usual microphone performance arrogance

nonetheless

the speaker   *acoustic assistanceless*

hhhhhh

hhhh

hhhhhhhh hhhhhhhha

mmmmhhhhhaaaa

haaaa haaaa

a a a

haaaa

h–

microphone interruption

        chitters

                speaker unties feet

                        STEP

                        stops

                                speaker looks down

                                        wet concrete stage

stagehands follow set plans   per contractligations
permits applied
pirouette as they slather and smooth
sign concrete hearts of passing fancies
and stone stage

speaker

wades thru   rapidly drying concrete

dries midstride   toe pointed   knee kicking back

concrete elegance

aaaah

aaaah   aaaahhhh   ha
aaaahhh ha hu

hu hu hu aaaah

aaahhhw   aaahhhw   aaahhhwwaah

ah

retaining arm movement is something

tho speaker

still feet still

still speaker still

remains still

aaahhh
wwaah

ah
ah
ah

ah

ha
ha

haw

hhhhaaawww aha h h h

w
w
wh wh

wha wha
whaaaa

hah

hha

ha

a second voice

full of obsessive verbal focus

without elocutionary imagination

in:

zzzz zzzz zzz zzzzzz

ZZZZZ UUPPPP

applause *audience roar*

"wasn't even formally listed"

"can't believe a live performance"

"if the venue had known. If they had just known."

BZZZZZ

ssssssSZZZZZZZ
UUUPPPPPP PPPP

guffaws & applause

anticipatory laughter

speaker tries cracking cement with fists

sometimes a lightfist is   just   the thing   but also

not

ssssss

SSSSSZZZZZUUUMMMMMMMM

a leatherclad fly loops and figure-eights around the speaker's head

note1: listed in playbill fineprint
note 2: leather is saville row stitched
for clients with inspired vision

divebombs the speaker pulls up a hair before impact

applause

fly lands gently on speaker's forehead

turns to face microphone

sszzzzz upppppsssssss

speaker attempts to lift arms
to flail
to flail intrusive fly from brow

fails flailing

deflates inaudibly

feet planted
keeping the speaker

swaying

weaving

fly dashes across wet concrete
leaving sixes of prints
drops   adds another six

compound eyes watching
the speaker watching   prints dry

fly descends

speaker throws an elbow
brings down a perfect five finger chop

fails to lift kick

panting
dribbling h's

the fly ZZZZing seamlessly through
grabbing a drip of moisture
a salt fleck
accumulated on the skin of
the weary speaker

classic exoskeleton verbal skeleton battle

zzzzzzzzzuuupppppp

h h h h

p h

h h h h

p p h h h

p h h h

p p h h h

p hhhh hhh ha

p p

p

ha ah

p p

h

pppp ppppp

p

hhha

pppppa

hh

pappppa ppa p p p ppa

happah

h zzz

pappppappppappppaaaa pap

p

p

p zz

pop

offstage stagehands share a thermos of coffee
orange cuplid handed between themselves
schlumping on steel beam hanging from rafters
waiting to rake away concrete imperfections

bookies roam aisles ineffectually
the betting odds dusty on chalk boards

the winning audience frothing
mink coat clouds
palm tree toupee breezes
drunk on champagne tsunamis

[*curtain*]

Act 3

Practice Controlled Biofeedback

speaker glides toward microphone

a new state of zen   all controlled breathing and in-the-momenting

a star pupil in the meditation pod

a wellness industry protégé   full of b-vitamins and sleepguilt

innnnnhaaaallle

h

mmuhmm
a haa

ah h h a h
mmuhmm

a h a h a h

hhhhhhh hhaaa hhhuummmm

h h h a h a

ha a ha ah
hhuum hmm

ahh hmm

hhhhhhha h a a a aaaaaa h

muhmm

mmuhmm

mmuhmm
hhhhuuuuuuummmm
a

hhhhhhhhaaaaaaaa

m

speaker   eyes closed   resettles

deep exhale

reapproaches brimming with propolis and

homeopathic verve

hhhhahhhahhha

hhhahhahahahhhhha

ha hah
haha ha

h h h

a giant squid critic's skeptical tentacle flings *down from rafters*

deep sea impatience

dripping from pulsating suckers

pooling salty at speaker's feet

giant squid critic wraps a taut tentacle *around speaker's waist*

a firm squeeze and a tuck and

khkhkhkhk

hhhhuuuup

giant squid critic scoops speaker straight up

to splintered rafters

speaker remains   inert

giant squid critic flips speaker upside down
a shake & a tweak

assorted phonemes tumble

from speaker's strained mouth & linted pockets

giant squid critic senses sufficiency

a final familiar squeeze tentacular luck

places speaker in front of microphone

upside down

sssqquuueeeeeeek

eeeeeeeekkkk hhhhaa

eeeeeeekkkkaaaah

giant squid critic   resets speaker   feet   centrestage

pats speaker's head   firmly

shuffles speaker toward microphone

a final firm pat on the small of the speaker's whiskering spine

h aa a
h aa h

ahhhh hha

ahhhhh hhaah

ahhhh

ahhhhh hha

hhhha hhaah

hhaaa

hhhhhhuuuuuuuu

hhhhhhuuuup hhhhhhuuuuuuuu

hhhhhhuuuuuuuu

ppp p p p

giant squid critic taps tentacle tip stageleft

drumming an impatient rhythm

hhhha

hhahhaa

hhhha

hhahhaa

hhhhha

hhhhha

hhhhhuuuuuppppp pp pppp pp p

hhahhaa

hhhhha

hhahhaa

hhhhha

hhahhaa

p

giant squid tentacle shoots back to rafters

can't help someone whose biofeedback loop is wired not
to accept help
thinks the giant squid tentacle   remembering deep sea wisdom

hhhh-p

[*curtain*]

Act 4
Avoid Thoughts that Produce Self-Doubt

standoff between microphone & speaker continues

spectator impatience wafting their way   curling through
thickening air

delicate smokethreads refusing   customary dissipation

speaker approaches microphone expectantly

this time

this time will be

the

time

mental note: a bird in the hand is terrifying

m   m   m   m m

h   h   h   m   m m

next time

perhaps

hhheepp hhhheeeeppp hhhhheeeepp

hep hep hep

hhhhheeeeppppp ppp pppp pppeppp ppppepppp

pppuuppp ppppupp pupppup ppuppppup

ppp ppp

hhheeeppp

ppp

pp

spotlight on figure in eleventh row   throatclears and gasps from
other patrons

figure sits with perfect posture   pinneat and pressed
hair waved expertly

figure sports her finest lillian gish   but remains discernibly
speaker's mother

cccrrroooooop

cccrrroooooop

ccccrrrooooo

p

speaker shuffles stageleft   *knocks mic stand*

squealing screechspirals punctuate the shuffle

ccrrrroookkk rooookkk

cccrorroookkssssskkkk

cccrrroookkkkhhhhsskk

cccrroookkkhhhsskkk
crohsk
crohusk

husk husk husk

s

k

speaker's mother deadpans   holds her own titlecards   the usual

New haircut?

speaker shuffles farther and farther stageleft   sidles the stage

edge with a pintaught toe

Not everyone needs to be quite so

speaker dips toe over edge of stage

a threat? minor resistance?

Though you are looking
a little comfortable
at your trough

speaker's mother furrows

homes in

It's never too late to join debenhams' training programme

speaker swings feet over orchestra pit   waits it out

What are you going to do about your obscene cashew budget?

speaker digs in eyes closed *still sees titlecards*

lowgrade closedcaptioning for nagging

[*curtain*]

Act 5

Connect With Your Audience:

smile

make eye contact

be a sympathetic figure

that doesn't make everyone

uncomfortable

– or –

Intermission:
It Pays to Advertise

speaker rolls out series of starjumps and gluteal fishsquats

there is a kind of jumping jack that only the best mettle can muster

the speaker dare not attempt such a jumping jack today

but one day

maybe

hahahah hahahha   ahhaha   hhhhhhut

hhhh
hhuuuuuuuttt

hhhhhuuuuuttttttt ttttt ttttt t

speaker   mid-burpee   is ensnared by

an impatient hashmark

the dear hash has been waiting in wings   eversolong

tapping his delicate serifs with increasing fury

nothing worse than a hashmark with brittle patience

t huuuuttt

tah tah tahhhhh
hhhhuuuutttt

hashmark storms stage

rolls speaker out of the way

for speaker's own good

speaker collects shards of shattered gumption and holler

positions tentative   toe on the jagged stagetape   marking
speaker's place

with regained composure wee hashmark shuffles downstage

the whiff of not having lost but certainly
not having won

pops open metal lunchbox withdraws seranned sandwich
commences munching

contemplating the performance's odds of trending scanning for
marketing opportunities

t
huuuuttt

tah tah tahhhhh hhhhuuuutttt

t huuuuttt

tah tah tahhhh hhhuuuuttt

one of the speaker's t's drifts off the lip   falls to the boards
with clatter

scurries over to the hash   hellbox solidarity

pulling a cheese crumble out of his pocket

to nibble on the way

t huuuuttt

[*curtain*]

Act 6

Be Prepared: Practice Practice Practice

speaker opens mouth

shuts mouth

gulps

throatpuffs   a swish

a fish in
a fish out

that old peanut

primed and shelled speaker paces

a boxer stepping up confidence

rhythmic lefts and rights square
the circle

up on tipped toes

fup fup fup

toward the microphone

throws a right

fhoowhoo   all air

duck
weave

watching for feedback upperhooks

opponent remains aloof

roped & doped silence

a chest puffed visualises success   as advised

by toastmaster alumni

and public relations experts

on the crumb of a scandal   with well-worded denial
bouquets

the speaker

spits mouthguard

the elocutioner

vowels like a

butterfly

consonants like a b

wwwahhhhh

wwaahhh   hhhaaa   hhooossshhh

wwwaaahhhhhhaaahh

whhooooosssshhhh

whaaaa whaaa whaaahaaaa whoooossh
whaaaa whaaa whaaahaaaa whoooossh

hhhhhhaaahh

practice makes

speaker turn off microphone

generating an impromptu live
rehearsal space   silent & expectant

speaker unfurls scroll

eyes bat poise

zeeeep babaha zeepzeepzeep

zrrrreeeepph

padascreeesp p p

speaker gesticulates   lets the hands have it

digitflutter   effortless silence

speaker spins and tutters   circles resting microphone

a performance for the ages

microphone turns itself on

[*cue applause*]

bbbbbbbbs   huh u hu h

ffffffssssss

speaker

drops
onto
stool

pours
water

towel
over
head

ducking tongue
weaving lungs

tee kay oh'd

[*curtain*]

Act 7

Focus on the Enjoyment You Are Providing Others

speaker skips toward microphone

bright   *readied*

hhh   hhh   hhhuuuuhhhhaaaw

hhha
aaw

hhhaaawwww

wahh   whaa   whaaaaa

wa-haa wa-
haaha

whoo   whoo   whoo

whoooosh

whoooo   sh
sh

shwhooo   sh

shwooo sh sh
shwooo shh   shhh

sh   sh   sh   haah

speaker shakes it off

tries to fail better

wonders: is there a better way to fail?
does it involve flailing? falling?
a fling? a flip?

a fwhip?

fffwhhuuuppp

whooha ha whhooowhhhooohh sh

whoooohhha sh sh sh

whooo whooo whooo

w-hoo w hoo w
wa hoo wa hoo

wha hoo sh wha hoo

sh

speaker sways rhythmically

maybe this is good enough   maybe
this is probably good enough

speaker settles into the moment

deciding to be good enough
mind over

mime

mime?

a mime in the wings

a mime trapped in a glass box   classic mime heckle

speaker shakes off mime heckler

one is good enough probably
one is probably good enough
probably enough good

probably

speaker covers eyes

feels around for microphone

whoo   ha ha

whooo ha ha

shhhh

speaker peeps between clamped fingers

the mime heckler means business
the mime heckler means faded jeans and black berets
the mime heckler means baguette clichés will be burned
henceforth
the mime heckler means never having an oyster in your
pocket when you need one
the mime heckler means real estate prices will burst
scattering agent confetti glistening
in sunlit streetview
the mime heckler means

the mime heckler wraps throat in gloved fingers

the universal sign for choking

the universal sign for mime hecklers

leading to the mime heckler wracking
ribs with mimey laughter

whwhooo   hhhwhoo   whooo

speaker turns body away from
the mime heckler

whhooom

whooo whoooo mmmm whooo   m

the mime heckler fishes   evokes a fully sunny day
so effectively the audience hears

the mime heckler's imagined birds

whhoooohhhsh whooo   hhhsh

speaker shuffles farther away
from the mime heckler

the mime heckler conjurs an oversized cane
fit for purpose

indicates pulling speaker offstage

speaker involuntarily dances
toward the mime heckler

the mime heckler puts more muscle
into the conjured hook

speaker sprawls across stage

skitters on cracked elbows
and kneecaps the rest of
the way

[*curtain*]

Act 8
Limit Caffeine & Sugar Intake

spotlight up centrestage

speaker stationed stageleft   well outside lightcircle

enter legohaired middlemanager rolling into spotlight
in an office chair

wheels across gloss & board   spins a wide circle   rolls over
speaker's anchored foot

daisies back to spotlight   creaks to halt

backdrop charts unroll
exposing the productivity of speaker
in pies and bars and reiterating in
downward-trending lines

speaker takes piechart to the face

[*roll laugh track*]

lego middlemanager is joined by two lithe backup chair
dancers

pinstriped yesmen   *creaky rhythm*
no sense for blocking

even with business degrees purchased from the finest
institutions

arms up   *roll left two counts*

speaker muddles
out of the way

roll right two counts   *spin*   *arms out*

speaker dodges a far left

legomiddlemanager joins yesmen   *links arms*

the three dancers sway as graphs and bars envelop speaker

spotlight fades down

[*cue applause*]

[*curtain*]

Act 9

Visualise Success: Don't Focus on What Could Go Wrong

lights up

speaker lies out   pinstraight

centrestage

playing dead

trick microphone

like it's a territorial bear

microphone stares ahead deadpan

waiting

silence continues

speaker inches stageleft everso

creeping away from expectant microphone

hits marks closest to wings two more steps then homefree

speaker trips on a pebble

rolls a softshoe tumble recovers

inspects pebble

there's much to admire smooth edges and discretion
a good pebble by all accounts

speaker tosses pebble in air
catches it against odds and again

a successful attempt to win over audience with limestone
simplicity

whhiiish

whhiiiishhh wwwhhhiiissshhooop

whoooossshhhheeepp whoosshheep

whoosshheeep

speaker spins on heel

a twist *a twirl* *a trip tripped*

netless

a second pebble

repeat

whoosshheep klink

whoosshheep kkkklink
whoosshheep kliiiiink
whoosshheep klinnnnnk
whoosshheep klinkkkkk hashweep

kliiinkha kkliiinkha   kkliiinkha

shweep

speaker juggles pebbles

comforting limestone klink

third pebble
complicates the toss

audience gasps enthralled

a cheer even

a reasonable entertainment

despite playbill deviance

speaker bows pleased
at last

a large boulder stageright

spins a half rotation

stage board cricks

the speaker looks up

drops

pebbles

one
two
three

the boulder

rotates

a half rote   inquisitive

'nother half rote

a raised granite brow

narly rote

the speaker realizes
futility of

boulder pleas

emergency geologists

juggling acumen

speaker

pivots

bows

cue larger boulder

rolls

head-to-toe

over speaker

[*roll laughtrack*]

[*curtain*]

Act 10

You May Benefit from More Intensive Therapy

speaker and microphone sit awkwardly *across from couples*
therapist

speaker fidgets *frigid fingers patterning* *awkward air*

supplying a peppy downbeat

couples therapist smiles serenely   makes notes   uses eyebrow
to coax speech

advances

sonic inks   blot

vibrating lines of blue

psychedelic circles   red   yellow

crackling whites on black

humpback whale matings

baby triumphantly throwing yogurt bowl to floor

aging lothario crying over lost erections

fbi agents eavesdropping on sound poets in the 50s
(groovy)

couples therapist presses

click

a cat's meow

neither patient twitches

click

static feedback

neither patient clears throat

speakerclack

speakerclack

speakerclack cricklecrack

huh whoo

huh whoo

inbreath

whoo huh

out

huh whoo

in

whoo huh

out

time elapses

timer dings

therapist makes note

same time next week

[*curtain*]

Bow

speaker shuts eyes

microphone hushed

speaker

in

out

in

out

still

[*blackout*]

Appendix I
Glossary of Selected Utterances

GLOSSARY OF SELECTED UTTERANCES

aaaahhh ha hu: denoting the tendency to. denoting the latter half of. denoting the reflection upon. denoting the denotation of denoting. Pronunciation guide: aspirated fumbletglitches. chilly not chilled

cccrrrroooooop: for pinning wings, closely monitored. Pronunciation guide: glottal whisperklitch and hit the oooooo smooth then cricklecrack glide it for the homestretch

eeeeeeeekkkk: mistlecroak at dawn. then the next dawn, then the next. all the wherefores one could count. Pronunciation guide: smallpocketed throatgloat. but not like that

h h h h h: in its pupal state, a noun. curiously stalwart in the face of willetblocking mollets, wittering kwillucks notwithstanding. Pronunciation guide: seek the muscular and cartilaginous of the squawkbox within

hhup: tehteh post pitpop. iced teeth. quick padma. Pronunciation guide: quockquock here quockquock there

hhuuup: a rinsed pudding potpotted. shhhh. Pronunciation guide: standard quockquock plus headtilt

khkhkhkhk: if a whelk walks it whalks whallandly. if a whelk whelks it whelks its whalk to the fit of agility. if a whelk wells it whells. if a whelk whens it whats just as easily. if a whelk whirls it whirls its spiralling gastropod heart out. if a whelk whelks at all. Pronunciation guide: a husky volume on the head will set the shoulder frame

pppppa: a favourite expletive of the Victorian gentry. falling out of fashion with the rise of the 8-hour workday, it was generally used when trying to sundress a raw prawn. Pronunciation guide: damply wheezed directly into the ear from behind unsuspecting target

ppp p p p: when you think you've had enough but. when you think it's all it can be but. when you think it can't but. when you when but. but then again. but. Pronunciation guide: froth it from the roots up. not hot froth unless delineating degrees of peevishness. a gentle seafoam should do in most circumstances

tah tah tahhhhh: a twiptwilk flumflop. flitterflup tumbletum. you know, a fliptip tripletwulk. whittled down to nothing. not nothing nothing, but nothing, you know? Pronunciation guide: milqued shorts and longs. Put some lung into it

uhh haaa: an awakening butterfly. hoarsewinged and plucktwitched in perpetual vellication. Pronunciation guide: crisp and throaty gossamer

wwwaaahhhhhhaaahh: theoretically, a possible. Pronunciation guide: caution recommended

zzzzzzzzzuuuppppp:

in music: a sonic moment captured within a lipid bubble of refracted colour

in medicine: the sound of a hardworking nerve ending unwinding after a long day

in real estate: with reference to present market conditions, connotes cosy spaces into which a serial renter will yet again learn to fit

in popular parlance: syn. tight. as in, "that beatnik bee's beat game is zzzzzzzzzuuuppppp"

in budget zoology: refers to a platypus' snort (most often of derision).

Pronunciation guide: simpering gutterping from the belly deep with a pinch of pinch (*exception*: not accurate for usage in questionable zoological research contexts, where a willing platypus would be your best guide)

Appendix II
Dramatis Personae

DRAMATIS PERSONAE

Speaker: hhh uhhhh hhhhuuh hhhuuh hhhhaaaaaaaaah h h h   h   h   h   h   h

Microphone: A stoic seen-it-all-before stringbean. "Call me Mic." Will flipflop for a crisp whiskey tumbler after hours.

Leatherclad Fly: Some may call him pretentious – a Musca domestica blockhead who's overgrown his Savillestitched trousers. But really, he's working hard to defy the crass dungpile stereotypes that have held him (and all flykind) back socially and professionally. There is no glass ceiling he won't sixprint given enough space to stretch his leatherclad wings.

Stagehands:

SH1: The most serious part of the job is definitely the lunch. A faulty sandwich will ruin the day. Not just the afternoon, but the morning too – all that time spent thinking about how everything will just fall out if it's not balanced tiptop. Sausage sandwiches (proper vegan ones), a dead win. But it's a balancing act. The main problem is that you're dealing with oblongs and rounds. Some will say just use a bakedforpurpose bap – then you'd be limebreezy oblongs and oblongs. But. A common bap? Never. What you need is the delicate embrace of a sprouted English muffin to cradle your vegan tubemeats (as the carcass lobbyists legally require us to call it). A kiss of balsamic tomato reduction. Maybe a streak of Dijon if you're 'handing for something feisty. Don't even look at me if you're going to forget the pinkpickled onion ribbons.

SH2: I guess they've been calling me Gherkin for a while now. Can't really remember. I must like gherkins.

Bookies: Nice boys, really. Don't put down what you can't afford.

Audience/Patrons: Full of verve and tittling excited whisperfishes. Eager to twitter in the foyer during intermission. Many have stoles.

Patrons' Stoles: The usual woodland creatures represented. Some are faux. Of those, half will readily admit it. Which fifty are you in?

Giant Squid (Critic): As the old saying goes, GSC is as wise as a disembodied appendage from the depths.

Figure in Eleventh Row (Speaker's Mother): The Speaker's therapist's files are sealed on this matter.

Impatient Hashmark: Honestly, this rascal is just trying to catch a break. Displeased that his theatrical debut has been punctured by the star never getting onscript.

One of the Speaker's T's: Well, if the Speaker isn't going to thrashup and get to it…

Mime Heckler: Six years Julliard. Graduate thesis on *Bouffon and the Contemporary Clown.* Some lean busking. Big break. Wine (red, good vintage). Red wine. Wine. Wine wine wine. Comeback. WMM award (Paris). Headtotoe believes he can save any production.

Legohaired Middlemanager: The middle is where it's at. Inexpressibly delighted to be in a position to make the lives of eleven people below the bar in this office miserable. A regular achievement tallied in a daily gratitude journal.

Lithe Backup Chair Dancers: Eager to be away from the office for the day. Can't help but cliptick clackclick their keyboards in pleasant beetle synchronicity to pass the punchin-punchout. Years of church basement practices finally pay off.

Yesmen: Mostly the backslapper kind. Unless there are apples to be polished. Pinstripes a little too loose, as if tailored for someone else, or possibly stitched before they pulled the deflate tab on their shoulders for just the right level of slight inward crumple. Quietly resentful of the new HR inclusivity policy to rename their department Yespeople.

Boulder: Family dates back to the Pleistocene and he'll never let you forget it.

Couples Therapist: Doesn't even need to look at a clock anymore–she can just *feel* life pass by in 50-minute bickered increments.

Post-script
by a rawlings

The Nerves Centre: Post-Script

In her play *Identity: A Poem*, Gertrude Stein wrote, "And so to turn excitement and not nervousness into a play.... Let us try" (Stein and Dydo 1993, 589). Szczepaniak twists Stein's call-to-arms by turning nervousness and not excitement into a play. A deep dive into scripted performance, general anxiety disorder, and performance anxiety, *The Nerves Centre* breaks down the seeming effortlessness of approaching the microphone, inviting playfulness into the difficulty inherent in tackling performance-related anxiety.

Szczepaniak's *Nerves* centres the script in her poetic sights. Structurally, *Nerves* relies on conventional script typesetting – roman for speech, italics for stage directions noting physical movement. The script is divided into ten acts. There are characters, curtains, blackouts. But when performance is partnered with a close study of anxiety disorders, poetic play disorders scripted convention. Szczepaniak not only casts performance and anxiety in lead roles; as author, she choreographs language itself in typographic bounds and plotted twists across each recto-verso spread.

All ten act titles double as nods to self-help guides for folks seeking to address anxiety issues. We enter the script with the first act's interrogative title: "Act Natural." With this, she places centrestage theatrical terminology that has been adapted to colloquialism. The oxymoron of these two words establishes the tension that will unfold over the long performance poem. Subsequent titles survey a how-to for the sufferer of performance anxiety – "Connect with Your Audience," "Be Prepared: Practice Practice Practice," and "Visualise Success" to note a few.

At the outset of the poem, a speaker and a microphone are juxtaposed in the first line. The microphone itself becomes a player in the room – not solely a manipulatable object or prop that supports the human actor, but instead an agential actor itself: "usual microphone performance arrogance" (p. 15). Here, Szczepaniak assigns an anthropomorphizing trait to a human-produced entity (the microphone), revealing through adverb the taut relationship between the human and non-human players: anxiety/arrogance. Szczepaniak extends the human-nonhuman conundrum through the introduction of the word 'speaker'. Is the speaker the human character previously introduced, or the non-human appendage of the microphone? The speaker, despite having feet, remains still (p. 20).

While the speaker is a consistent, focal character throughout the acts with the microphone playing a support role, the poem is populated with comic incidental characters against whom the speaker attempts to exorcise anxiety. An errant technical crew is conjured at the end of Act Two, segueing into Act Three's tentacular electrical cords. The speaker's mother appears in Act Four in a non-speaking role, though she manifests her criticisms through oversized title cards held in the theatre space. Act Ten finishes with a couples' therapist who navigates the relationship between speaker and microphone. The title cards and couples' therapist flaunt Szczepaniak's strength in writing humour as a coping mechanism.

But what of *performing* anxiety – how English language functions in relation to semantics of often slowed to aphasiatic speech of someone undergoing a panic attack? In Szczepaniak's hand, language itself undergoes an anxiety attack. She manifests the inarticulatable, the imponderable, in her *ooh*'s, *ahh*'s, and *eee*'s. Scripted, a performer invites proto-semantic utterances to erupt from her body. After a comedic scripted non-spoken introduction, speech is indicated as a series of choreographic h and a's – which offers a multitude of entry points for director or performer: laughter, breathy frustration, microphone hiss (what a catty asshole!). Szczepaniak's phonemic explosions extend page after page after page. *H*'s and *a*'s involve *m*'s, and eventually *w*'s (*whaaaa*) leading into *z* and the eventual formation of the morpheme '*sup*.' The astute reader, the reader not reading between the lines but between the pages, receives the satisfying discovery of the elongated 'What's up?' being delivered through this tortuous sound poetry work by page 22. Anxiety colours the easiest, unthinking, tip-of-tongue interjections with extraordinary difficulty.

In the act titled "Avoid Thoughts that Produce Self-Doubt," Szczepaniak focuses speech acts on the phonemes *p* and *k*. Plosives such as *p* are the antagonist of any mic check, but she disallows her potential actors from avoiding the doubt on mic-craft that can arise when dealing with a hot mic prone to plosive outbursts. Partnering *p* with *k*, Szczepaniak gives her speaker vocal acrobatics oscillating between labial *p*'s and glottal *k*'s.

In the act titled "Focus on the enjoyment you are providing others," I delighted in what I read as auto-poetic utterances Szczepaniak embedded in her text. The voiceless fricative *sh* dominates speech acts; notably, the *sh* pronunciation is proffered in the author's last name, represented by the Polish digraph *sz*. The act also mentions birds, with the visual shape of *w* and *m* (the other two dominant phonemes/ideogrammes) winging their ways through the overcast sky of each page. "The enjoyment you are providing others" – as I understand

Szczepaniak is a self-confessed ornithophobe, her insistence on including birds in a play on anxiety is comedy incarnate.

Also phonemically noteworthy: Act Six asserts in its speech acts the electrical into a buzz and pop of phonemic *z*, *p*, *s*, and *b*. And as the climax of the play's narrative arc, Act Eight: "Limit Caffeine & Sugar Intake" contains no spoken elements. Perhaps the nutrition advice worked to soothe the act's verbal diarrhea during panic.

With a surfeit of recent poetry publications materializing around mental health, disease, and medicalization, *Nerves* is a welcome self-assessment salve or salvo – a mediation, meditation, interrogation of how language performs in a body anxious of performing language anxious of performing body anxious of languaging, anxious of anxiety. Where Fiona Templeton asserted in *You: The City* that "Theatre is the art of relationship" (Templeton 1990, 139), Szczepaniak focuses on the relationship with the performed, performing, strained, observed self in the little theatre of literary genre hybridity she has innovated.

WORKS CITED

Stein, Gertrude, and Ulla E. Dydo. 1993. *A Stein Reader.* Evanston, Illinois: Northwestern University Press.

Templeton, Fiona. 1990. *You, the City.* Roof Books. https://books.google.co.uk/books/about/You_the_city.html?id=pR9aAAAAMAAJ&pgis=1.

ACKNOWLEDGEMENTS

I have so much gratitude for so many *Nervey* things:

Jason Camlot–endless thanks for editing *Nerves* so beautifully, precisely, generously, and with humour that really found the *Nerves* joy.

Too many thankyous to the Angelas Hibbs & Rawlings–Rawlings for time and energy and reading and wit, and especially for writing the thoughtful afterword. Hibbs for virtual drives through snow, pithy book reviews, reading and sharing early drafts, and knowing exactly when to deploy a well-placed "meh."

Many thanks to everyone at DC, but especially to Keith Henderson and Philippe Barey (such beautiful marginwork, Phil!).

Rory Waterman & Francesca Hardy–for all things Nottingham, and to Rory especially for the recurring invitation to talk to your classes.

Kate & everyone at Tough Mary's and Rebecca & Asher at Pelham Kitchen–thanks so much for the incredible welcoming second homes.

And most of all, Hendrix Szczepaniak & Jamie Popowich–both incisive *Nerves* critics, lovers of puns and running jokes and photocollages. Special thanks to Hendrix for "peanut butter toes"–her first and longest running non-slapstick conceptual joke that's hiding somewhere in the *Nerves.*

Angela Szczepaniak is the author of *Unisex Love Poems* (an illustrated novel-in-poems) and *The QWERTY Institute* (visual fictions), which details the lives, inks, and deep-C adventures of a variety of fonts as they wade through awkward social situations. She is a Lecturer and Programme Director of the MA in Creative Writing at the University of Surrey and lives in London.